FORWARD/COMMENTARY

The National Institute of Standards and Technology (NIST) is a measurement standards laboratory, and a non-regulatory agency of the **United States Department of Commerce**. Its mission is to promote innovation and industrial competitiveness. Founded in 1901, as the National Bureau of Standards, NIST was formed with the mandate to provide standard weights and measures, and to serve as the national physical laboratory for the United States. With a world-class measurement and testing laboratory encompassing a wide range of areas of computer science, mathematics, statistics, and systems engineering, NIST's cybersecurity program supports its overall mission to promote U.S. innovation and industrial competitiveness by advancing measurement science, standards, and related technology through research and development in ways that enhance economic security and improve our quality of life.

The need for cybersecurity standards and best practices that address interoperability, usability and privacy has been shown to be critical for the nation. NIST's cybersecurity programs seek to enable greater development and application of practical, innovative security technologies and methodologies that enhance the country's ability to address current and future computer and information security challenges.

The cybersecurity publications produced by NIST cover a wide range of cybersecurity concepts that are carefully designed to work together to produce a holistic approach to cybersecurity primarily for government agencies and constitute the best practices used by industry. This holistic strategy to cybersecurity covers the gamut of security subjects from development of secure encryption standards for communication and storage of information while at rest to how best to recover from a cyber-attack.

Why buy a book you can download for free?   We print this so you don't have to.

Some are available only in electronic media. Some online docs are missing pages or barely legible.

We at 4th Watch Publishing are former government employees, so we know how government employees actually use the standards. When a new standard is released, an engineer prints it out, punches holes and puts it in a 3-ring binder. While this is not a big deal for a 5 or 10-page document, many NIST documents are over 100 pages and printing a large document is a time-consuming effort. So, an engineer that's paid $75 an hour is spending hours simply printing out the tools needed to do the job. That's time that could be better spent doing engineering. We publish these documents so engineers can focus on what they were hired to do – engineering. It's much more cost-effective to just order the latest version from Amazon.com

If there is a standard you would like published, let us know. Our web site is usgovpub.com

Many of our titles are available as eBooks for Kindle, iPad, Nook, remarkable, BOOX, and Sony eReaders. Buy the paperback from Amazon and get Kindle eBook FREE using MATCHBOOK. Go to https://usgovpub.com to learn more.

Why buy an eBook when you can access data on a website for free? HYPERLINKS

Yes, many books are available as a PDF, but not all PDFs are bookmarked? Do you really want to search a 6,500-page PDF document manually? Load our copy onto your Kindle, PC, iPad, Android Tablet, Nook, or iPhone (download the FREE kindle App from the APP Store) and you have an easily searchable copy. Most devices will allow you to easily navigate an ePub to any Chapter. Note that there is a distinction between a Table of Contents and "Page Navigation". Page Navigation refers to a different sort of Table of Contents. Not one appearing as a page in the book, but one that shows up on the device itself when the reader accesses the navigation feature. Readers can click on a navigation link to jump to a Chapter or Subchapter. Once there, most devices allow you to "pinch and zoom" in or out to easily read the text. (Unfortunately, downloading the free sample file at Amazon.com does not include this feature. You have to buy a copy to get that functionality, but as inexpensive as eBooks are, it's worth it.) Kindle allows you to do word search and Page Flip (temporary place holder takes you back when you want to go back and check something).

Most eBooks are available for FREE under the Amazon Matchbook Program when you purchase the paperback.

Visit **USGOVPUB.COM** to learn more.

NIST Special Publication 800-205

Attribute Considerations for Access Control Systems

Vincent C. Hu
David F. Ferraiolo
D. Richard Kuhn

C O M P U T E R   S E C U R I T Y

National Institute of
Standards and Technology
U.S. Department of Commerce

NIST Special Publication 800-205

Attribute Considerations for Access Control Systems

Vincent C. Hu
David F. Ferraiolo
D. Richard Kuhn
Computer Security Division
Information Technology Laboratory

June 2019

U.S. Department of Commerce
Wilbur L. Ross, Jr., Secretary

National Institute of Standards and Technology
Walter Copan, NIST Director and Under Secretary of Commerce for Standards and Technology

Authority

This publication has been developed by NIST in accordance with its statutory responsibilities under the Federal Information Security Modernization Act (FISMA) of 2014, 44 U.S.C. § 3551 *et seq.*, Public Law (P.L.) 113-283. NIST is responsible for developing information security standards and guidelines, including minimum requirements for federal information systems, but such standards and guidelines shall not apply to national security systems without the express approval of appropriate federal officials exercising policy authority over such systems. This guideline is consistent with the requirements of the Office of Management and Budget (OMB) Circular A-130.

Nothing in this publication should be taken to contradict the standards and guidelines made mandatory and binding on federal agencies by the Secretary of Commerce under statutory authority. Nor should these guidelines be interpreted as altering or superseding the existing authorities of the Secretary of Commerce, Director of the OMB, or any other federal official. This publication may be used by nongovernmental organizations on a voluntary basis and is not subject to copyright in the United States. Attribution would, however, be appreciated by NIST.

National Institute of Standards and Technology Special Publication 800-205
Natl. Inst. Stand. Technol. Spec. Publ. 800-205, 42 pages (June 2019)
CODEN: NSPUE2

This publication is available free of charge from:
https://doi.org/10.6028/NIST.SP.800-205

Certain commercial entities, equipment, or materials may be identified in this document in order to describe an experimental procedure or concept adequately. Such identification is not intended to imply recommendation or endorsement by NIST, nor is it intended to imply that the entities, materials, or equipment are necessarily the best available for the purpose.

There may be references in this publication to other publications currently under development by NIST in accordance with its assigned statutory responsibilities. The information in this publication, including concepts and methodologies, may be used by federal agencies even before the completion of such companion publications. Thus, until each publication is completed, current requirements, guidelines, and procedures, where they exist, remain operative. For planning and transition purposes, federal agencies may wish to closely follow the development of these new publications by NIST.

Organizations are encouraged to review all draft publications during public comment periods and provide feedback to NIST. Many NIST cybersecurity publications, other than the ones noted above, are available at https://csrc.nist.gov/publications.

Comments on this publication may be submitted to:

National Institute of Standards and Technology
Attn: Computer Security Division, Information Technology Laboratory
100 Bureau Drive (Mail Stop 8930) Gaithersburg, MD 20899-8930
Email: sp800-205-comments@nist.gov

All comments are subject to release under the Freedom of Information Act (FOIA).

Reports on Computer Systems Technology

The Information Technology Laboratory (ITL) at the National Institute of Standards and Technology (NIST) promotes the U.S. economy and public welfare by providing technical leadership for the Nation's measurement and standards infrastructure. ITL develops tests, test methods, reference data, proof of concept implementations, and technical analyses to advance the development and productive use of information technology. ITL's responsibilities include the development of management, administrative, technical, and physical standards and guidelines for the cost-effective security and privacy of other than national security-related information in federal information systems. The Special Publication 800-series reports on ITL's research, guidelines, and outreach efforts in information system security, and its collaborative activities with industry, government, and academic organizations.

Abstract

This document provides federal agencies with a guide for implementing attributes in access control systems. Attributes enable a logical access control methodology where authorization to perform a set of operations is determined by evaluating attributes associated with the subject, object, requested operations, and, in some cases, environment conditions against policy, rules, or relationships that describe the allowable operations for a given set of attributes. This document outlines factors which influence attributes that an authoritative body must address when standardizing an attribute system and proposes some notional implementation suggestions for consideration.

Keywords

access control; access control mechanism; access control model; access control policy; attribute considerations; attribute; assurance; attribute-based access control (ABAC); authorization; privilege.

Acknowledgements

The authors, Vincent C. Hu, David F. Ferraiolo, and Rick Kuhn of the National Institute of Standards and Technology (NIST), wish to thank their colleague Isabel Van Wyk, who reviewed drafts of this document. Additionally, the authors would like to thank Mr. Art Friedman (NSA) and Mr. Paul Jacob (Booz Allen Hamilton, Linthicum, MD) for initiating this effort. The authors also gratefully acknowledge and appreciate the comments and contributions made by government agencies, private organizations, and individuals in providing direction and assistance in the development of this document.

Patent Disclosure Notice

NOTICE: The Information Technology Laboratory (ITL) has requested that holders of patent claims whose use may be required for compliance with the guidance or requirements of this publication disclose such patent claims to ITL. However, holders of patents are not obligated to respond to ITL calls for patents and ITL has not undertaken a patent search in order to identify which, if any, patents may apply to this publication.

As of the date of publication and following call(s) for the identification of patent claims whose use may be required for compliance with the guidance or requirements of this publication, no such patent claims have been identified to ITL.

No representation is made or implied by ITL that licenses are not required to avoid patent infringement in the use of this publication.

Executive Summary

Access control systems that use attributes are capable of enforcing a broad range of access control policies. Attributes enable precise access control and allow a large number of discrete inputs into an access control decision. They also provide an extensive set of possible combinations of those variables to reflect rules to express policies.

Attribute-based access control systems rely upon attributes to not only define access control policy rules but also enforce the access control. Attributes need to be established, issued, stored, and managed under an authority. Attributes shared across organizations should provide assurance via location, retrieval, publication, validation, update, modification, security, and revocation capabilities. Consequently, all attributes must be established, defined, and constrained by allowable values required by the appropriate digital policies; successful deployment of the schema for these attributes and allowable attribute values must be completed to help enable subject (e.g., consumers) and object (e.g., protected resource/service) owners with policy and relationship development.

Once attributes and their allowable values are established, methods for provisioning attributes and appropriate attribute values to subjects and objects within a framework for storing, retrieving, updating, or revoking attributes must also be established. In addition, interfaces and mechanisms must be developed or adopted to enable sharing of these attributes. Finally, to achieve the assurance of attributes, an Attribute Evaluation Scheme, which brings confidence based on the five principal areas of interest, needs to be established:

Preparation refers to the planning of an attribute creation and sharing mechanism, as well as rules for maintaining attributes' privacy between attribute providers and access control functions. This consideration should be based on the business operation requirements to meet the goal of efficiency and confidentiality of operations.

Veracity establishes the policy and technical underpinnings for semantic and syntactic correctness of subject, object attributes, or environment condition, and ensures that the obtained attributes are trustworthy based on the agreed upon or trusted definitions, protocols, measurements, and maintenance processes of attributes.

Security considers different standards and protocols used for secure transmission and repositories of attributes between systems in order to avoid compromising the data integrity and confidentiality of the attributes or exposing vulnerabilities in attribute providers, access control functions, or other types of malicious actions performed by unauthorized entities.

Readiness refers to the frequency of refresh for attributes that change. The system must ensure that attribute update and retrieval frequencies adequately support access control enforcement functions. This capability also ensures that a recent set of attributes required for appropriate access control for the protected objects in question is cached in the event that the most current attributes from authoritative sources or repositories cannot be accessed during an information system emergency (e.g., low bandwidth, loss of service). In addition, the fail over and backup capability of attribute repositories need to be considered.

Management provides mechanisms for maintaining attributes to ensure the efficiency and consistent use of attributes, including metadata, hierarchical structures for attribute grouping, minimization and transformation methods for attribute performance, and additional support capabilities (e.g., attribute integration with authentication, logs for recording attribute access and updates).

NIST Special Publication (SP) 800-162, *Guide to Attribute Based Access Control (ABAC) Definition and Considerations* [1], introduced guidance on access control definitions and considerations for the implementation of access control systems but did not include detailed recommendations on considerations such as the preparation, veracity, security, readiness, and management of attributes. This document aims to provide federal agencies with a guide to attribute considerations with Attribute Evaluation Scheme examples for access control. The Attribute Evaluation Scheme should be determined by an enterprise information system's requirements, and the enterprise information system should validate these requirements to realize the appropriate organizational attribute evaluation scheme capability in line with performance and cost recommendations. Note that this document does not establish a universal attribute scheme that suits all business capabilities and performance requirements; instead, it provides considerations and examples that can be adapted to meet the specific needs of an organization when defining its attribute evaluation scheme.

Table of Contents

List of Appendices

List of Figures

List of Tables

1   Introduction

1.1 Purpose

Virtually all authorization systems are dependent on attributes for rendering access control decisions and ultimately enforcing policy over subject access requests to system objects.

Perhaps the most deployed authorization scheme in use today is role-based access control (RBAC), where roles (e.g., manager, accounts receivable clerk, loan officer) provide a means of expressing a subject's authority, responsibilities, or job functions. The process of assigning a role attribute value to a subject indirectly grants the subject permissions that are associated with the role. An emerging alternative to RBAC is to grant or deny subject requests to access system objects based on enterprise-specific attributes of subjects and objects and, optionally, environment conditions and policies that are expressed in terms of those attributes. This approach to access control is commonly referred to as attribute-based access control (ABAC). Subject names and groups, as applied in access control lists, are other examples of attributes used in formulating access policies and computing decisions.

Access control systems typically encompass four layers of functional and information decomposition—enforcement, decision, access control data, and administration—involving several components that work together to bring about policy-preserving access. At its core is a policy decision point (PDP) that computes decisions to permit or deny subject requests to perform operations on system objects. A policy enforcement point (PEP) both issues requests and accepts PDP decisions that are based on the current state of the access control data, which comprises access control policies expressed in terms of attributes and attribute values. These values may, for example, pertain to the attributes of a subject seeking access and the attributes of a target object. Policies and attributes are managed through one or more Policy Administration Points.

Regardless of the type of authorization scheme being deployed, confidence in access control decisions is dependent on the accuracy, integrity, and timely availability of attributes. If a subject is inappropriately assigned an attribute value, whether through complacency, error, delay, or malice, the result is the same—an inappropriate access state.

Over past decades, a variety of approaches have emerged for storing, managing, and applying attributes. One approach is to tightly couple policies and attributes with the PDP. Consider Next Generation Access Control (NGAC) [2], an ABAC standard where both policies and attributes are managed through policy-preserving configurations of a standard set of elements and relations that may reside in PDP memory. An eXtensible Access Control Markup Language (XACML) deployment may provide a more distributed approach. Policies are expressed as extensible markup language (XML) documents that are locally loaded into PDP memory from a policy retrieval point and evaluated with respect to attributes that are remotely retrieved from one or more policy information points. In another deployment, attributes are stored, managed, and shared (exchanged) across a multitude of relying parities, each with their own PDP and policy store.

The approach used for storing, managing, and retrieving attributes is significant due to the relative risk factors involved. An authorization system with local attributes affords a closed protection boundary in which attributes never need to be exposed to the outside world. In a deployment where attributes are stored, managed, and retrieved from remote systems, attributes are susceptible to the management and protection strategies of those systems and to the networks that are used to transfer attributes.

Due to the variability of access control system types and deployments, this document generically focuses on attribute properties—**preparation, veracity, security, readiness**, and **management**—that should be considered for instilling confidence in the use of attributes in computing access control decisions and enforcing policy. This document outlines factors that influence attributes which an authoritative body must address when standardizing attribute evaluation systems and proposes some notional implementation suggestions for consideration.

This document extends the information in 1) NIST Interagency or Internal Report (NISTIR) 8112, *Attribute Metadata: A Proposed Schema for Evaluating Federated Attributes* [3]; 2) NIST Special Publication (SP) 800-162, *Guide to Attribute-Based Access Control (ABAC) Definition and Considerations* [1], which defines ABAC's terms and concepts and discusses considerations for ABAC implementation; 3) NISTIR 7316, *Assessment of Access Control Systems* [4], which demonstrates the fundamental concepts of policy, models, and mechanisms of access control systems; 4) NISTIR 7874, *Guidelines for Access Control System Evaluation Metrics* [5]; and 5) NIST SP 800-178, *A Comparison of Attribute-Based Access Control (ABAC) Standards for Data Service Applications* [6], which describes XACML and NGAC and then compares them with respect to five criteria.

Note that while not the focus, assumptions and dependencies on authentication of access control subjects are addressed.

1.2 Scope

The intended audience for this document is an organizational entity implementing access control solutions where there is an expectation of sharing attributes with or accessing information from other organizations. This document does not prescribe internal attribute evaluation system standards that an organization may need in their enterprise systems or within a community other than the organization itself. Rather, the focus is on the establishment of confidence in attributes applied to an organization's access control implementation.

1.3 Audience

This document assumes that readers are familiar with access (authorization) control and have basic knowledge of operating systems, databases, networking, and security. Given the constantly changing nature of the information technology (IT) industry, readers are strongly encouraged to take advantage of other documents—including those listed in this document—for more current and detailed information.

1.4 Document Structure

The sections and appendices presented in this document are as follows:

- Section 1 states the purpose and scope of attributes used for access control systems.

- Section 2 gives overviews of the basic abstractions of access control attributes: *subject attribute*, *object attribute*, and *environment condition* in a working environment.

- Section 3 discusses the considerations for attributes from the perspectives of preparation, veracity, security, readiness, and management.

- Section 4 demonstrates a general attribute framework with an example for integrating and defining attributes to achieve the attribute veracity.

- Section 5 demonstrates the mapping of attribute considerations to the Attribute Evaluation Scheme with examples of different applications and explains the use of the Attribute Practice Statement.

- The Appendix lists additional information on the XACML translation of the Office of Management and Budget (OMB) Memorandum M-07-16 privacy rule in a general attribute framework.

2 Consideration Elements

Access control systems using attributes can enforce a broad range of access control policies. Attributes—given by a name-value pair—contain characteristics of the subject, object, or environment conditions, thereby enabling precise control, allowing for a higher number of discrete inputs into an access control decision, and providing a larger set of possible combinations of those variables to reflect a wider and more definitive set of possible rules to express policies. In addition to the earlier work documented in NIST Special Publication 800-162 [1] and OMB M-04-04 [7], which suggested attribute implementations applied to the subject and object and environment conditions within an ABAC system, general attribute considerations need to be addressed based on the following definitions.

Access Control Functions are functions for an AC mechanism or scheme. For example, the Extensible Access Control Markup Language (XACML) [6] scheme architecture includes functions such as Policy Decision Points (PDPs), Policy Enforcement Points (PEPs), Policy Administration Points (PAPs), and Policy Information Points (PIPs) as defined in International Organization for Standardization/International Electrotechnical Commission (ISO/IEC) 29146:2016, along with some logical components for handling the context or workflow of policy and attribute retrieval and assessment. Access control functions hosted in local or network systems (called *local* or *remote access control function*, respectively) must function together to provide access control decisions and policy enforcement.

An **Attribute Provider** is any person or system that provides subject, object (or resource), or environmental condition attributes to access control functions or other attribute providers (in such cases, the attribute provider is called a *remote attribute provider*), regardless of transmission method. An attribute provider may be the original authoritative source or act as an intermediary between the authoritative source and the access control function by receiving information from an authoritative source and then re-packaging the attributes for delivery/routing to storage repositories of access control function or attribute provider. Attribute values may be human-generated (e.g., an employee database), derived from formulas (e.g., a credit score), or system-generated (e.g. environment conditions such as time, location, etc.).

Regardless of the source of attributes, an *access control function* should ensure that the attributes associated with the subject, object, or environment condition to which they apply are secure and error-free to the best of its ability. Attribute proofing by the defined scheme from which organizations can make risk-based decisions is based on the confidence in attributes supplied by an access control function, attribute provider, or local attribute resource. Figure 1 illustrates the scope of attributes used, including authentication, authorization, and attribute proofing. Note that the remote attributes are those provisioned through remote networks.

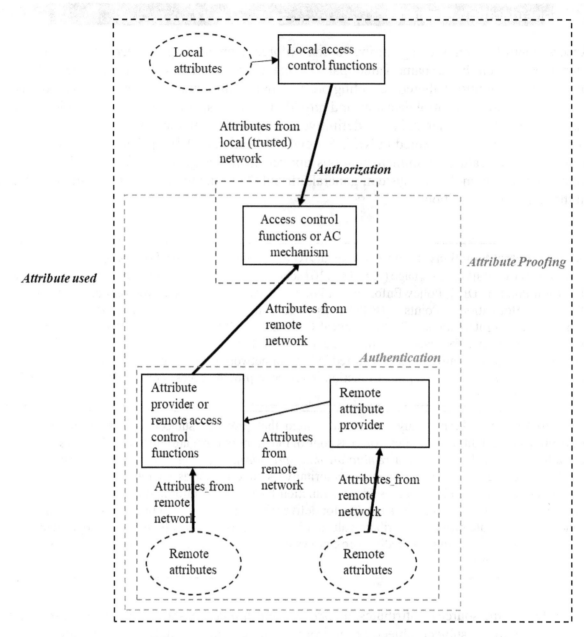

Figure 1: Scopes of attributes used: Authorization, Authentication, and Attribute Proofing of an access control system

3   Attribute Considerations

Access control relies upon the evaluation of attributes to not only define access control policy rules, but also enforce the rules. Good, reliable, and up-to-date attribute data that support appropriate, well-informed access decisions are essential. Thus, attributes provided by an access control function or attribute provider need to be assured through an attribute proofing mechanism. Attributes must identify, define, and describe a set of criteria and standards that can be used to determine the attributes that are used for access decisions.

Once the authoritative sources define the appropriate attributes and allowable values, methods need to be established to provision appropriate attribute values to subjects and objects with a framework for communicating, storing, retrieving, updating, or revoking attributes. In addition, interfaces and mechanisms must be developed or adopted to enable the sharing of these attributes. Finally, an attribute evaluation scheme needs to be established to bring confidence based on the five principal areas of interest:

Preparation refers to the planning of the attribute creation and sharing mechanism as well as rules for maintaining attribute privacy between attribute providers and access control functions. This consideration should be based on the business operation requirements to meet the goals of efficiency and confidentiality of operations.

Veracity establishes the policy and technical underpinnings for semantic and syntactic correctness of subject, object attributes, or environment condition and ensures that the obtained attribute values are trustworthy based on the agreed upon or trusted definitions, protocols, measurements, and maintenance processes of attributes.

Security considers different standards and protocols used for secure transmission and repositories of attributes between systems in order to avoid compromising the data integrity and confidentiality of the attributes; exposing vulnerabilities in attribute providers, access control functions, or entities; or other types of malicious actions performed by unauthorized entities.

Readiness refers to the frequency of refresh for attributes that change. The system must ensure that attribute update and retrieval frequencies adequately support access control enforcement functions. This capability also ensures that a recent set of attributes required for appropriate access control for the protected resource in question is cached in the event that the most updated attributes from authoritative sources or repositories cannot be accessed during an information system emergency (e.g., low bandwidth, loss of service). In addition, the fail-over and backup capabilities of attribute repositories need to be considered.

Management provides mechanisms for maintaining attributes to ensure the efficiency and consistent use of attributes including metadata, hierarchical structures for attribute grouping, minimization and transformation methods for attribute performance, and additional support capabilities (e.g., attribute integration with authentication, logs for recording attribute access and updates).

3.1 Preparation Consideration

Attributes shared across organizations should be assured for all uses, including attributes that are located, retrieved, published, validated, updated, modified, secured, and revoked. Consequently, all attributes must be defined and constrained by allowable values required by the appropriate policies. The schema for these attributes and allowable attribute values must be published to all participants for use in rule and relationship development. Attributes may be created and shared by multiple organizations. Therefore, the design of an attribute framework must consider the federated usage, creation mechanism, and maintenance scheme according to the business and access control requirements. Attribute providers and access control functions also need to maintain privacy to meet the confidentiality requirement. Minimizing the number of attribute sources used in authorization decisions may improve performance and simplify the overall security management of the access control solution. In addition, organizations planning to deploy an access control solution may benefit from establishing a close working relationship among all of the organization's stakeholders who will be involved in the attribute preparations.

3.1.1 Subject Attribute Preparation

Attribute authorities typically provision subject attributes for the type of attribute provided and managed through an access control function or attribute provider, except for non-person entities (NPE) such as autonomous services or applications generated or controlled by operating systems. There are typically multiple authorities, each with authority over different subject attributes. For example, *security* might be the authority for clearance attributes, while *human resources* might be the authority for *name* attributes. Subject attributes that require assured information sharing to allow subjects from one organization to access objects in another organization must be consistent, comparable, or mapped to allow equivalent policies to be enforced. For example, a member of organization *A* with the role *Job Lead* wants to access information in organization *B*, except organization *B* uses the term *Task Lead* to denote the equivalent role. Table 1 shows an example of a subject's attributes.

Table 1: Subject attribute example

		Policy Applied[a]
	ID numbers (e.g., Organization A)	Subject and Administrator object access
Division	Division name (e.g., Software Development Division)	Subject and Administrator object access
Group	Group name (e.g., Testing group)	Subject and Administrator object access
Name	Person's name (e.g., Joe Smith)	
Role	Role ID (e.g., Job Lead, (or Task lead))	Administrator object access
	Training label (e.g., Minimum Requirement)	Administrator object access

^a Policy Applied column lists the type of policy rules which require this attribute for the evaluations of access permission if multiple policies are applied to the access control system.

As subject attributes may be provisioned by different authorities (e.g., *human resources*, *security*, *organization leadership*, etc.), methods for obtaining authoritative data must be regulated. For example, only *security* authorities should be able to provision and assert *clearance* attributes and attribute values based on authoritative personnel clearance information; an individual should not be able to alter his or her own clearance attribute value. Other subject attributes may involve the subject's current tasking, physical location, and the device from which a request is sent. Processes need to be developed to assess and assure the quality of such subject attribute data.

In addition, authoritative subject attribute provisioning capabilities should be appropriately dependable for privacy and service expectations. These expectations may be detailed in an Attribute Practice Statement (APS), which provides a listing of the attributes that will be used and may identify authoritative attribute sources throughout the organization. Still, additional network infrastructure capabilities are required to share and replicate authoritative subject attribute data within and across attribute providers and access control functions.

3.1.2 Object Attribute Preparation

The data or resource owner/custodian of access control function or attribute provider typically provisions object attributes upon object creation. For example, object attributes may be bound to the object or externally stored and referenced via a metadata service and repository. While it may not be necessary to have a common set of object attributes in use across the enterprise, object attributes must be consistently employed within an individual system to fulfill access control policy requirements, and available sets of object attributes should be published for those wishing to mark, tag, or otherwise apply object attributes to their objects. At times, it might be necessary to ensure that object attribute data are not tampered with or altered (i.e., remain static) to satisfy an access request. Table 2 shows an example of an object's attributes.

Table 2: Object attribute example

Object attribute Name		Policy Applied^a
	ID numbers (e.g., 234567)	Subject and Administrator object access
Object owner	Name of object owner or organization (e.g., Organization B)	Subject and Administrator object access
Object creation date and time	Date and time (e.g., May 26, 2015)	Subject and Administrator object access
Object deletion date and time	Date and time (e.g., May 26, 2017)	Subject and Administrator object access
	Authorization level (e.g., 1)	Administrator object access
		Administrator object access

^a Policy Applied column lists the type of policies which require this attribute for the evaluations of access permission if multiple policies are applied to the access control system.

Access control authorities may not be able to appropriately and closely monitor all events. Frequently, object information is driven by non-security processes and requirements according to business cases for the consumer clientele in question. Measures must therefore be taken to ensure that object attributes are assigned and validated by processes that the object owner or administrator considers appropriate and authoritative for the application. For example, object attributes must not be modifiable by the subject to manipulate the outcome of the access control decision. Objects can be cryptographically bound to their attributes to identify whether objects or their corresponding attributes have been inappropriately modified. Mechanisms must be deployed to ensure that all objects created are assigned the appropriate set of object attributes to satisfy the policy used. It may be necessary to have an Enterprise Object Attribute Manager to coordinate these requirements. Object attributes must be made available for retrieval for access control decisions. Additional considerations for creating object attributes include:

- In general, subjects may not know the values of an object attribute (e.g., what the security level is or who can access the object). Data confidentiality of object attributes should be accounted for so that authorized subjects only see the values that are applicable to them.
- As with subject attributes, a schema is required for object attributes defining attribute names and allowed values to ensure object attributes are valid within its semantics and syntax definitions.
- Attribute values need to remain consistent within policies that share the attributes.

There have been numerous efforts within the Federal Government and commercial industry to create object attribute tagging tools that provide not only data tagging, but also cryptographic binding of the attributes to the object. These capabilities also provide validation of the object attribute fields to satisfy access control decision requirements. For example, Global Federated Identity Privilege Management (GFIPM) [8] specification provides the attribute data model for subjects, and the National Identity Exchange Federation (NIEF) [9] specification provides a collection of attribute definitions developed with the intent to enable organizations to exchange attribute data.

3.1.3 Attribute Granularity

For an access control mechanism to support the principle of least privilege, constraints must be placed on the attributes that are associated with a subject to further reduce the permissible capabilities. The organization-specific least privilege policy is described by specifying the access control rules, and the access control systems provide various specifying methods which achieve different degrees of granularity, flexibility, scope, and different groupings of the controlled objects for the least privilege policies. This involves the granularity of object attributes (e.g., data field) that an access control system can control. For example, this feature enables privacy control for information with different classifications in the data fields of a record. In addition, some access control systems are required to control or manage end-point system components such as servers, workstations, routers, switches, guards, mobile devices, firewalls, email, antiviruses, databases, and web applications. Thus, it is important to consider the granularity of attributes based on the organization's requirements and system architecture.

3.1.4 Environment Condition Preparation

Environment condition refers to context information that is generally not associated with any specific subject or object but is required in the decision process. Environment conditions are different from subject and object attributes in that they are not administratively created and managed prior to run-time but, rather, are intrinsic and must be detectable by the access control function for use in access decisions. The access control function evaluates environment conditions such as the current date, time, location, threat, and system status against current matching environment variables when authorizing an access request. Environment conditions drive access control policies to specify exceptional or dynamic rules that supersede those rules driven only by subject or object attributes. When composing access control rules with environment conditions, it is important to ensure that the environment condition variables and their values are globally accessible, tamper-proof, and relevant to the environments in which they are used.

3.1.5 Consideration Examples

Table 3 shows example criteria of attribute preparation considerations.

Consideration	Criteria	Applied Attributes
Attribute Coverage	Attributes cover all protection policy requirements of the organization (i.e., semantically complete).	Subject, Object
Attribute Governance		Subject, Object, Environment condition
Attribute Granularity	Attributes are based on the organization's security and operation requirements.	Object

3.2 Veracity Consideration

With the exception of NPE, the veracity of an asserted attribute is affected by the care that the access control function or attribute provider takes in obtaining, evaluating, and maintaining the value while in possession of it. Two characteristics that influence *veracity* include:

- Attribute trustworthiness
- Attribute accuracy

3.2.1 Attribute Trustworthiness

Attribute trustworthiness considers how well the sources of attributes are authenticated, identified, and validated. This applies to the attribute source from the remote attribute provider or access control function. There is a distinction between truthfulness of the attribute's value and authoritativeness of information. However, the focus must be on access control function or attribute provider's trust (e.g., credentials, federation relations) that the attributes represent the underlying subject, object, or environment condition. For example, the attribute value of a specific credit score may be disagreeable, but the attribute user may trust that it came from a specific credit reporting agency. Table 4 shows an example of attribute trustworthiness based upon different levels of confidence.

Table 4: Attribute trustworthiness examples

Levels of confidence	Based On		
	Self-reported		
Medium	Attribute proofing (mostly for subjects)		
High	Derived from independent of underlying factors (i.e., original source)	High identity proofing (mostly for subjects)	Authenticated source with service level agreements (SLAs)

Attribute trustworthiness proofing relies on a concept by which organizations can make risk-based decisions based on trust in attributes supplied by remote access control functions or attribute providers. Approaches to achieving this purpose include:

- Identify, define, and describe a set of standardized attribute metadata that can be used by access control functions to help determine confidence in the attributes they are leveraging for authorization decisions.
- Identify, define, and describe a set of criteria that can be used to determine the trustworthiness of attributes (e.g., shown in Table 4), which may include a scoring system mechanism to determine an objective confidence level for a given attribute.
- Develop suggested performance guidelines and specifications for remote access control functions or attribute provider operations based on an organization's risk tolerance.

For remote subject attributes (i.e., not from local access control function itself or NPE), attribute assurance relies on the chain of trust used to determine and report on the attributes. If the remote access control function or attribute provider reporting the attributes did not verify them, then it is necessary to provide a chain of evidence that shows that the attributes were authoritatively verified and that their association with the relevant system has been maintained.

3.2.2 Attribute Accuracy

Given the broad spectrum of entities that will interoperate with each other, synonyms of attribute definitions are inevitable. Interoperability standards and protocols that all entities agree to are therefore essential to enabling cooperation. Agreed-upon standards in both syntactic and semantic attribute values must be developed to ensure successful interoperation of systems. For example, a consideration is that a relying party (RP) may be assured that an attribute came from a trusted credit reporting agency, but the attribute value of a specific credit score may be disagreeable. Thus, dictionaries with standardized syntax and semantics for attribute namespaces need to be agreed upon and published by the access control functions or attribute providers.

Attribute value inaccuracy results from different data types (e.g., integer, string, Boolean) or different classifications (e.g., levels, ranks) between access control functions and attribute providers. Thus, agreement, federated mitigation, or interpretation/conversion may be required such that the attribute value is accurate for the policy evaluation. For example, attribute values that are intrinsic to the access control model (e.g., roles for RBAC systems) must be accurately assigned to the subjects who are associated with the organization's business functions. Unless the access control function or attribute provider is responsible for the standard, algorithm, or protocol that generates the attribute value, accuracy is typically evaluated with the attribute trust as described in Sec. 3.2.1.

3.2.3 Consideration Examples

Table 5 shows examples of consideration of attribute veracity criteria.

Consideration	Criteria	Applied Attributes
	Attributes are properly verified for veracity through provision and management.	Subject, Object, Environment Condition
	Documented rules or standards exist for attribute value assignment and definition (syntax and semantic rule).	Subject, Object
	Criteria can be used to determine the trustworthiness of attributes.	Subject, Object
Remote Access Control Function/Attribute Provider Guideline	Performance guidelines and specifications exist for remote access control functions or attribute providers.	Subject, Object

NISTIR 8112, *Attribute Metadata: A Proposed Schema for Evaluating Federated Attributes* [3], reviews the accuracy, provenance, currency, privacy, and classification of veracity in terms of standardized attribute metadata used by organizations to support business decisions. The document enables enterprises to leverage automated decision support systems that rely on attributes to implement a broad range of essential business functions. It also provides a guide for establishing a scoring framework and its associated components to enable standardized attribute confidence scores.

Section 4 demonstrates a general attribute framework with an example for integrating and defining attributes to achieve attribute veracity. The example shows an organization, initially started from NLP, which governs multiple access control systems in an enterprise environment.

3.3 Security Consideration

Access control functions and attribute providers must ensure a number of properties: the security of an attribute's value and its metadata, freedom from tampering or corruption, adequate vetting of stored attribute information, and a high level of protection within its enclave. Attribute security also determines how securely the access control function or attribute provider supplies attributes to an access control function. In other words, how does the access control function or attribute provider ensure that the attribute it intends to send is the one that the access control function will actually receive? Attribute security includes evaluating security for both stored attribute and transmitted attribute conditions. For example, to improve the security of attribute transmission, attributes can be sent via an encrypted and signed mechanism (e.g., a signed SAML [10] assertion, TLS [11]).

3.3.1 Stored attribute

Stored attribute security evaluates the mechanism for the actual attribute store and how well the access control function and attribute provider protect the information or attribute-generation processes. Note that stored attribute security ensures the generation and management of an attribute and its value while the attribute value consideration, as described in Sec. 3.2.2, focuses on the semantic accuracy of attribute values. Factors or capabilities that must be evaluated include:

- Encryption
- Measures taken to detect unintended alteration of attribute values
- Data stores on a network behind a proper defense-in-depth posture
- Policies enforced on the attribute update, copy, revoke, or modify process
- Logged and audited change of attribute

The stored attribute factors or capabilities are commonly used to evaluate the local access control function because the required information can be rendered locally. However, for the attribute provider, remote access control function, or remote attribute provider without local access to the involved systems, an agreement or contract that contains checklists for the evaluation of the factors or capabilities might be required.

3.3.2 Transmitted attribute

Transmitted attribute security evaluates how securely the attribute is transmitted to the attribute provider or access control function. Factors or capabilities that must be evaluated include:

- Security protocols are used for transmitting both attribute requests and attribute values to the attribute provider or access control function (e.g., transmitting in the clear without encryption versus PKI-enabled TLS sessions).

- Replay attack protection is typically accomplished by including information provided by the access control function into the signed message that is provided by the remote access control function or attribute provider. This guarantees the integrity and confidentiality of the attribute.

- Transmitted attributes are applied in a multi-tier receipt of attributes (i.e., when attributes are sent by remote access control function or provider such that the assured attribute can be passed through the chain of forwarding routes). For example, for higher levels of assurance, using digitally signed attributes (crypto-binding) provides a hash of the attribute to ensure that it has not been altered or tampered with before it is received.

In addition to the access control function and attribute provider's transmission security, the security arrangements between access control functions must be considered. In order to make a correct policy decision, the transmission of attributes between access control functions should be protected from change by any other internal process of the system. If applicable, a set of consideration elements or schemes (e.g., SAML) should be identified that can be used by the access control system to help determine whether the attributes have demonstrated considerations for security criteria.

3.3.3 Consideration Examples

Table 6 shows example considerations for attribute security criteria.

Table 6: Example considerations for attribute security criteria

Consideration	Criteria	Applied Attributes
Repository security	Secure or trusted attribute repository (e.g., dedicated or shared attribute repositories)	Subject, Object, Environment Condition
Communication security	Secure communication between access control functions and attribute providers (e.g., encrypted)	Subject, Object, Environment Condition
	Transmission of attributes between access control functions are protected from change by any functions	Subject, Object, Environment Condition[1]
Non-repudiation capability	Methods for non-repudiation of attribute transmission	Subject, Object, Environment Condition[1]
Attribute change policy	Formal rules, policies, or standards to create, update, modify, and delete attributes	Subject, Object, Environment Condition[1]

3.4 Readiness Consideration

Attribute readiness considers the quality of attributes with respect to refresh, timing, cache, and backup capabilities, all of which allow access control to process the accurate access permissions without errors caused by out-of-date or unsynchronized attribute information.

3.4.1 Refresh

Access control functions need information on how often an attribute's value is pulled or obtained, as well as how securely the attribute's value is processed when it is needed. Readiness considers how attribute values are updated or validated—*refreshed*—against ground truth by the access control function or attribute provider. Proactive acquisition must be considered for the impact of a refresh rate on a specific attribute (e.g., whether the information is being pushed from another source to the access control function or attribute provider or pulled on a schedule proactively). Attribute values on a schedule or on-demand give assurance of how current and, therefore, how applicable the attribute value may be.

3.4.2 Synchronization

Synchronization of attribute transmission sequences between access control functions must be coordinated based on the sequence of the access control system's processing scheme or protocol such that the updates of attributes and their values will not result in faulty access control decisions. For example, to keep access control functions in sync in the XACML [12] scheme, updating attributes by policy administration point (PAP) should not be allowed while an authorization process is in progress; updated or newly added attributes will be available after policy enforcement points (PEPs) finish the process.

---

[1] If the environment condition is human-controllable or machine-generated instead of non-human controllable factors such as time, location, and temperature.

3.4.3 Cache

Readiness also ensures that a recent set of attributes required for appropriate access control for the protected object in question are cached in the event that the most updated attributes from authoritative attribute sources or repositories cannot be accessed during an information system emergency (i.e., low bandwidth, loss of service). In addition, the failure recovery capability of attribute repositories must be considered.

3.4.4 Backup

Since attributes are the critical components of an organization's access control system, they should always be available while the system is functional. Readiness should therefore include the capabilities of fail-over and the recovery of attributes from the failures of attribute repositories or transmission systems.

3.4.5 Consideration Examples

A set of consideration elements that can be used to help determine the attributes' readiness is shown in the attribute readiness criteria example in Table 7.

Consideration	Criteria	Applied Attributes
Attribute refresh frequency	Attribute refresh frequency meets the system performance requirement.	Subject, Object, Environment Condition
	Attribute caching during run-time meets the system performance requirement and protocols between access control functions.	Subject, Object
Attribute process sequence	Attribute transmission between access control functions are coordinated without generating errors.	Subject, Object
		Subject, Object

3.5 Management Considerations

A number of factors should be reviewed to ensure the efficiency and consistent use of attributes. Management mechanisms include metadata, hierarchical structures for attribute grouping, minimization and transformation methods for attribute efficiency, and additional support capabilities such as attribute integration with authentication, delegation of attributes, attribute review, and logs for recording attribute access and updates as described in the following sections.

3.5.1 Group Attribute Use Metadata

In the course of managing attributes, metadata is applied to subjects and objects as extended attribute information useful for enforcing fine-grained access control policies that incorporate information about the attributes and manage the volumes of data required for enterprise attribute management. Metadata can also be used to assign an assurance level or measure of confidence as a composite score for attribute veracity [3], security, and readiness. Standardized attribute metadata are elements of information about each attribute. These elements include information about the attribute such as the value (i.e., how often it is updated), the processes used to create or establish the attribute (i.e., whether it is self-asserted or retrieved from a record), and the source of the attribute itself (i.e., authoritative). Regardless of the access control methodology, establishing a score system for an attribute's metadata elements can support access decisions. The decision to use specific attributes from remote access control functions or attribute providers could then be made based on individual attribute confidence scores.

Table 8 shows an example of standard (agreed-upon) metadata for sharing provenance information as *attribute source*. The specific attribute value "Person" may be sufficient for accessing data for a public information request but insufficient for access to a sensitive system since the metadata "Clearance Level" is self-reported and not drawn from an authoritative source.

Table 8: Example of standard attribute name/value for attribute source metadata

Standard Attribute Name	Standard Attribute Value
Entity applicability	Person
Name	Joe Smith
Classification	Public
Confidence Level	
Attribute from	USAJOBS.gov

To enhance access control flexibility and facilitate attribute management and administration, hierarchical relationships among groups and attributes are usually applied, such that instead of assigning each subject/object with the same attributes, the subjects/objects can be collected into groups with appropriate group metadata and values (i.e., meta-attribute) [13] which represent the common characteristics of the subjects/objects in the system. Group metadata can also be combined into a higher order group if a group of metadata possesses the same characteristics. Thus, a group hierarchy is a partial order relation where groups in the lower order obtain all attributes assigned to the groups at the higher order.

Figure 2 shows an example of a group hierarchy where attribute *Attribute_1* 's *ID = User Group_A* and *Attribute_2's ID = Group_B* belong to the metadata *Metadata_1*'s value: *ID = Support* and *Skill = Administration*. Metadata *Metadata_1* and *Metadata_2* inherit *Metadata_3*'s *ID = Production* and *Security Class =2*. So, if a subject has the attribute *Attribute_1*, it will also have attribute values of *Metadata_1* and *Metadata_3*.

16

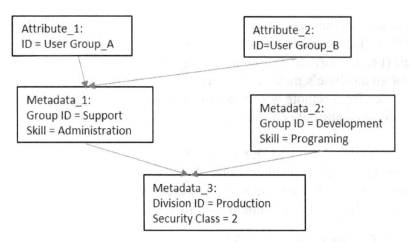

Figure 2: Group metadata

3.5.2 Attribute Privilege Hierarchies

Attributes can be classified in a tree structure based on their privilege relationship in an access control system. Such a relationship can be represented by attributes being the nodes in the tree, such that if a senior subject attribute is assigned to a junior subject attribute, then all the access privileges associated with this junior subject attribute are automatically acquired by that subject, which have the senior attribute through the attribute-value inheritance. Figure 3 (a) shows an example where subjects with the subject attribute *Role = Professor* also have the privileges of a subject with the subject attribute *Role = TA*. For object, if a senior object attribute is assigned to a junior object attribute, then all the access privileges associated with this senior object attribute are automatically allowed to access the objects with the junior attributes through the attribute-value inheritance. Figure 3 (b) shows an example where access to the object with attribute *Type = Secret* can also access the object with attribute *Type = Classified*.

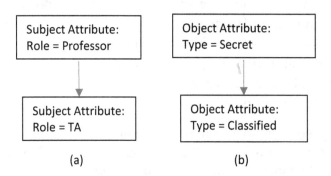

Figure 3: Attribute privilege hierarchies of subject (a) and object (b)

3.5.3 Attribute Transformation

Attributes that are typically assigned to very large numbers of subjects and many types of objects can lead to administrative difficulties from different perspectives for access control. For example, a cloud system may have many types of virtual machines, block storage resources, object storage resources (e.g., objects, containers, accounts), or network resources (e.g., firewalls, routers), all of which have many attributes of their own. As a result, there would be numerous attributes specific to different types of objects, and new attributes would be added to the system as new object types. Thus, it takes considerable effort to assign or de-assign these attribute values to subjects as well as objects. Furthermore, authorization policies defined with these attributes would be large and complex in nature and can result in difficulty with specification, update, modification, and review.

To manage these difficulties, the transformation of attribute management—such as reduction, expansion, and grouping as described in Sec. 3.5.2—must be considered. Attribute reduction transforms a large set of attribute assignments into smaller sets by abstracting attributes that are too specific for particular types of subjects or objects. Minimizing the number of attribute sources used in authorization decisions improves performance and simplifies overall security management such as creation, updating, deletion, the import or export of attributes, the design of modular authorization policies, and the modeling of hierarchical policies [14].

3.5.4 Integration with Authentication

The shift from internal to public-based hosting (e.g., cloud) and increasing numbers of subjects who access applications from outside of the organizational boundary have resulted in the increased distribution of applications. Attributes of subjects and objects can be associated with the identities of subjects and objects, making it efficient or required to trust the subject and object attributes provided by the authentication system through a secure connection for advanced authentication technologies such as federated digital identity or single sign-on (SSO). Attributes are specified in privileges and constraints of access control rules, and applications require more information than the identity of a subject (user), such as geolocation, time of day, role, organization, account information, and authentication details. In addition, a major benefit of integrating attributes to authenticated IDs and access control with the company's authentication system is to keep the cost and management objects under budget [5].

For example, XACML needs contextual information about the subject and, potentially, the object being accessed to properly evaluate an access request. With a standardized inbound identity protocol such as SAML (Security Assertion Markup Language, an XML-based framework for communicating subject authentication, entitlement, and attribute information), OAuth, or OpenID Connect, it is much simpler for the XACML deployment to leverage identity information in a standard way for fine-grained access-control attributes. More specifically, SAML provides a standard for conveying identity information to access control attributes by assuming two primary roles in any transaction: 1) the organization where the identity is established, known as the identity provider (IdP), and 2) the organization that will use this identity, known as the service provider (SP). The *assertion* is a trusted statement of identity established by a cryptographic key exchange that the IdP makes to the SP. The service provider and the identity provider will agree upon what information the SP will require as the *attribute contract*, which typically identifies the *subject* who is making the request. It can also contain other attributes that the SP needs to make the application work, especially for making access control decisions [15].

3.5.5 Delegation

Proper enforcement of data resource policies is dependent on the enforcement of attribute administrative policies. This is especially true in a federated or collaborative environment where governance policies require different organizational entities to have different and possibly overlapping responsibilities for administering attributes. A common practice is to restrict the creation of attribute values and subject and object assignments to those attributes in different venues based on a notion of mutual trust. A preferred and more rigorous approach for establishing and managing attribute administrative policies is through delegation. Delegation allows an authority (delegator) to delegate all or parts of its own authority or someone else's authority to another subject (delegate). This would enable a systematic and policy-preserving approach to the creation of administrative roles. The delegation of administrative capabilities begins with a single administrator and ends with subjects with attribute management capabilities. Delegation assumes a system that manages attributes through a standard set of administrative operations, applying a recognized enforcement interface and a centralized decision-making function as might be used for accessing data resources.

3.5.6 Attribute Review

Assigning one or more attributes to a subject indirectly grants the subject capabilities to perform various operations on system objects. Similarly, assigning an object to one or more object attributes indirectly establishes access entries to a variety of subjects to perform operations on that object. A desired feature of an access control system is to review these capabilities and access entries on an attribute-by-attribute basis or via combinations. This feature is sometimes referred to as "before the fact audit" and object discovery. "Before the fact audit" has been suggested by some to be one of RBAC's most prominent features [6], and it includes the ability to review the consequences of assigning a subject to a role. It also includes the capability for a subject to discover or see accessible objects prior to issuing an access request. The ability to review the access control entries of an object attribute is equally important. What are the consequences of assigning an object to an attribute or deleting an assignment? Another valuable review consideration is the identification of the attributes necessary for a subject to be able to access an object as well as what attributes might prevent such access.

3.5.7 Log

For more stringent security, an organization might require that all activities—including changes (e.g., creation, modification, deletion) and use of attributes—be logged in an audit trail providing approval of changes to attributes and values for later investigation. Further, monitoring of high-risk privileged access to high-risk attributes should be implemented. An annual re-certification of attribute validation schema may be required.

3.5.8 Considerations Examples

Table 9 shows example considerations for attribute management criteria.

Consideration	Criteria	Applied Attributes
	Attribute metadata, hierarchies, and inheritance schemes are accurate based on the access control policy requirements.	Metadata (meta-attributes)
Integration with authentication	Attributes are integrated into the company's authentication system for attribute federation, SSO, etc.	Subject, Object
Attribute efficiency	Attributes expansion and minimization improve the performance of access control system.	Subject, Object
Attribute delegation	Attributes are delegated based on the access control policies	Subject, Object
	Attributes assignments can be reviewed.	Subject, Object
	Attribute changes and access can be logged.	Subject, Object, Environment Condition

Based on the considerations in Sec. 3, Sec. 4 will demonstrate a *general attribute framework* for integrating and defining attributes using metadata. The example shows access control rules that were initially developed from NLP, which governs multiple access control systems in an enterprise environment.

4 General Attribute Framework

The preparation and veracity of attributes is especially crucial when applying access control to a multi-host environment, such as an enterprise system, where attributes are created and managed by diverse organizational units. The attributes are used for both local (organization unit) and global (enterprise) access control policies. Therefore, a mechanism is required to mitigate the syntactic and semantic differences of attributes. An example is the General Attribute framework (GAF) that allows attributes to be defined with syntactic and semantic accuracy across federated and networked systems under the enterprise ABAC domain where initial access control policies are in natural language without formal attribute definitions. This chapter reviews the use of GAF for attribute accuracy.

To enforce access control policies across the enterprise, the policies must be in a machine-readable format processed by the computer that performs access control for the information system (i.e., decision engine). However, most initial access control policies originate in natural language that cannot be ingested and processed by the decision engine. Thus, it is necessary to translate the natural language policies into machine-readable policy rules. A general approach is to have an object domain (e.g., laws or statutes for privacy policies) expert examine the system's subject attributes and map the access privileges to the system's objects according to the policy applied. After completion of the work, object domain experts will again be needed when the policy or the system is updated. Since each system requires the object domain expert's effort to translate the policy from its local attribute definitions, the total cost of the administrative overhead may be unmanageable.

This problem also applies to mapping between an enterprise attribute schema and an application-specific schema, particularly those built before the enterprise schema was defined and/or commercial off-the-shelf (COTS) products that come with their own built-in schema (e.g., those typically established for legacy information systems). For attribute accuracy, organizations must normalize subject attribute names and values or maintain a map of equivalent terms, all of which should be managed by a central authority.

It is, therefore, important to devise a portable framework that is general enough to be used by access control administrators to compose their access control policies without the extra cost of translating or learning object domain knowledge. A GAF should be constructed from the content and ontology of the intended policy using *generic attributes* which can be applied to the specific attributes of any information system in different application domains. The National Identity Exchange Federation (NIEF) Attribute Registry is a collection of attribute definitions that are intended for use by organizations and communities that wish to implement Federated Identity and Privilege Management technologies within the context of the NIEF. Each attribute definition listed there has been developed with the intent to enable organizations to exchange attribute data in a manner that permits machine parsing and comprehension [9]. Figure 4 shows the relations of the object domain policy and the machine-readable policy for each individual system.

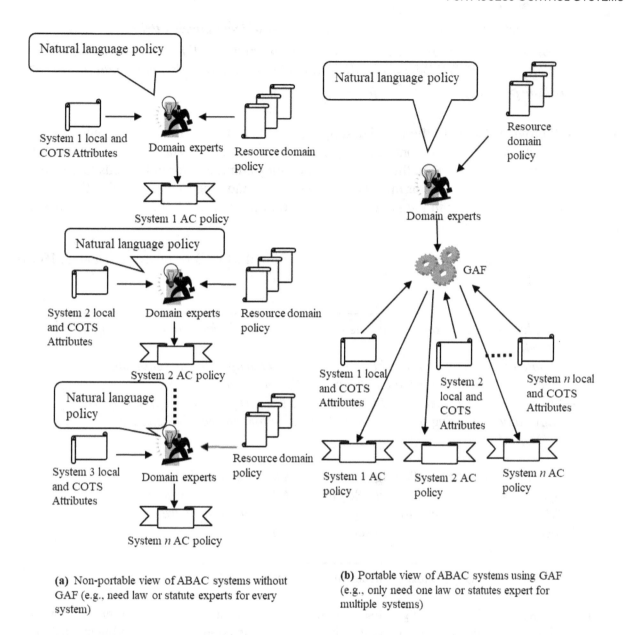

Figure 4: Producing access control policies without (a) and with a (b) General Attribute Framework (GAF)

The goal of a GAF is to provide a framework to serve as a layer between NLP and machine-readable policies and rules, allowing access control policy authors to compose policies without object domain expert knowledge of the policy related to the object. Derived from analyzing the content and ontology of the policy rules, a GAF contains access rules associated with the subject and object generic attributes, which are generic for any domain of an attribute-based access control (ABAC) system. In short, a GAF is an ABAC policy with rules in terms of generic attributes based on access control elements: subject/object attributes, environment conditions, and actions. The format of a GAF access control rule is:

IF <subject generic attribute $_1$> …….. AND/OR<subject generic attribute $_n$> AND
<environment condition 1>…..AND/OR <environment condition n>THEN ALLOW
<action $_1$> …….. AND <action $_n$> ACCESS TO OBJECT WITH <object generic
attribute $_1$> …….. AND/OR <object generic attribute $_n$>

A GAF will provide clear definitions and descriptions of the generic attributes by using a common vocabulary such that any access control policy administrator can understand them. To enforce the policy on the information system, the access control policy administrator only needs to assign the GAF's generic attributes as tags or metadata to the subjects and objects by reviewing the existing subject and object attributes in the system. There is no need to create policy rules since they are already embedded in the GAF.

Figure 5 lists part of the original text of privacy rules from the OMB M-06-16 [16] and OMB M-07-16 statutes [17].

"Implement protections for remote access to personal identifiable information"
(Step4)
"Implement NIST Special Publication 800-53 security controls requiring
authenticated, virtual private network (VPN) connection" (Step 4.1)
"Implement NIST Special Publication 800-53 security controls enforcing
allowed downloading of personally identifiable information" (Step 4.2)
---OMB M-06-16

Attachment 1 Safeguarding Against the Breach of Personally Identifiable
Information, Section C Security Requirement, Item: Control Remote Access:
"Allow remote access only with two-factor authentication where one of the
factors is provided by a device separate from the computer gaining access".
---OMB M-07-16

Figure 5: Original text of privacy rules from OMB M-06-16 and OMB M-07-16

Figure 6 shows a GAF containing a list of common generic attributes in columns for privacy statutes. The "computer" column contains the environment condition; the "subject attributes" column contains the generic attributes for the subjects; the "actions attributes" column contains the available actions; the "object attributes" column contains the generic attributes for the object; and the "audit" column lists the actions that must be performed after access is granted. For example, the first rule in Figure 6 states that a remote user employed by a federal agency and using two-factor (level 3) generic attributes is permitted to read objects with PII generic attributes. Note that the "computer" column contains the common generic attributes that are shared by the subject and object, and the "audit" column contains the obligation required after the access action is performed.

		Subject Attributes/Values		Object Attributes/Values	Audit
OMB M-06-16	Remote User	Employer = Federal Agencies Authentication Level = Two-factor (Level 3)	Permitted to Read		
OMB M-06-16	All	Employer = Federal Agencies	Permitted to Read/Write	Special Characteristics = Sensitive Data	Action (Audit) = All Data Data Extracts = requires verification that each extract, including sensitive data, has been erased within 90 days of its use
OMB M-07-16	All	Employer = Federal Agencies	Permitted to Read/Write	Data Tags = SSN	Write (Collect) = Minimum needed for agency function
OMB M-07-16	All	Employer = Federal Agencies	Permitted to Read/Write		Write (Change) = Corrections or notations agency Justifications Write (Collect) = Minimum needed for agency function

Figure 6: Example rules from OMB M-06-16 and OMB M-07-16

The following examples demonstrate the mapping to concrete instances of the OMB M-06-16 privacy rule GAF shown in Figure 6. Example 1 (Table 10) is for an information sharing center (ISC) in which the local subject and object attributes are assigned based on ISC's data formats. Example 2 (Table 11) is for a federal organization wherein the subject and object attributes originate from the Human Resources Department (HRD). These two examples show the portability property of a GAF for information systems with different domains. The "generic attributes" row refers to the generic attributes from the GAF, and the "local attributes" row shows the example system attributes that must be reviewed to decide the qualification (yes or no) of the mapped generic attributes. The GAF access control rule for the OMB M-06-16 rule is composed of all of the generic attributes in the row:

Grant Read *access for the user who has the attributes:* Remote User, Federal Agencies, *and* two-factor (Level 3) *to the resource data with the* PII *attributes.*

Example 1:

Attributes	Subject Attributes			Actions	Object Attributes	
Generic attributes	Remote Use	Federal Agencies	2-factor - level 3	Action		PII
Local Attributes	<Remote login ID>	Federation ID	Electronic Identity	Read	Vehicle Year	Vehicle Registration Number

Similarly, the following access control rule of the ISE can be achieved through the GAF:

Grant Read *access for the user who is* <Remote Login ID>, *has* Federation ID, *and* Electronic ID *to the resource data with the* Vehicle Year *and* Vehicle Registration Number *attribute.*

Example 2:

Table 11: Mapping of generic attributes of OMB M-06-16 rules to the HRD system of a federal organization

Attributes	Subject Attributes			Actions	Object Attributes
Generic attributes	Remote User	Federal Agencies	2-factor (level 3)	Action	PII
Local Attributes	<Remote Login ID>	Agency *HRD* ID	Remote Access key	Read	SSN

Similarly, the following policy rule of the *HRD* can be achieved through the GAF:

Grant Read *access for the user who is* <Remote Login ID> *and has* HRD ID *and* Remote Access Key *to the resource data with the* SSN *attribute.*

The XACML [12] implementation of the examples above is listed in the Appendix.

Note that to ensure the robustness of the GAF, the ontologies between the generic attributes may be expanded as they pertain to identified sub-rules or hierarchical relations of rules. Also, assertion-based policy rules appear in some policies, and the handling of these features must be addressed in the development of the GAF.

5 Attribute Evaluation Scheme

An attribute evaluation scheme should be determined by the requirements and capability of an organization while also considering risk, performance, and cost. This document does not intend to construct a universal scheme that suits all business requirements and capabilities. Instead, it provides mapping examples of scheme metrics for general access control systems which can serve as prototypes that may be adapted to meet the specific needs of an organization while it defines its attribute evaluation scheme.

5.1 Attribute Evaluation Scheme Examples

Table 12 illustrates an example of attribute evaluation scheme categorization based on considerations from previous discussions. Note that considerations may differ between systems or organizations, depending on their security requirements. As such, they should be assigned in conformance with the organization's operation and performance requirements and incorporated when relying on federated systems. Differences in levels between schemes should be considered for access decisions such as if an access decision uses two attributes, one in low and the other in high levels.

Table 12: Example of attribute evaluation scheme for attributes provisioned by remote access control functions or attribute providers

					Management
Level 1	Attributes cover all protection policy requirements of the organization (i.e., semantically complete)	Attributes are properly verified through provision and management	Secure attribute repository; secure communication between attribute providers and access control functions	Attribute refresh frequency meets the system performance requirement	Log for attribute changes and access
Level 2	Includes Level 1 preparation; attributes' standard procedures and creation, update, and revoking policies are defined and documented	Includes Level 1 veracity; documented rule or standards for attribute value assignment and definition (syntax and semantic rule)	Includes Level 1 security; dedicated attribute repositories	Includes Level 1 readiness; attribute caching during run-time meets the system performance requirement	Includes Level 1 management; attributes integrate with authentication
Level 3	Includes Level 2 preparation; attributes are under federated or unified governance	Includes Level 2 veracity; criteria that can be used to determine the trustworthiness of attributes	Includes Level 2 security; encrypted attribute values and communications between attribute providers and access control functions systems; methods for non-repudiation of attribute transmission	Includes Level 2 readiness; fail-over or back-up attributes support	N/A

					Management
Level 4	N/A	Includes Level 3 veracity; performance guidelines and specifications for remote access control function or attribute provider	Includes Level 3 security; transmission of attributes between access control functions should be protected from changing by any functions	Includes Level 3 readiness; formal rules, policies, or standards for logging the creation, updates, modification, and deletion of attributes	N/A

Note that as the characteristics of the three attribute types—subject, object, and environment condition—vary in different operational environments, their attribute evaluation schemes may be assigned by different criteria. This allows flexibility by compositing sets of schemes that are practical for assurance measurements. For example, the attribute evaluation scheme in Table 12 can be applied to an organization whose attributes may be supplied by remote access control functions or external attribute providers. This scheme is naturally different from what would be used for organizations that do not obtain external attributes, in which case a less restrictive consideration of scheme mapping is appropriate, as illustrated in Table 13.

Table 13: Example of attribute evaluation scheme considerations for object attributes not provisioned by remote access control function or attribute provider

					Management
Level 1	Attributes cover all protection policy requirements of the organization (i.e., semantically complete)	Attributes are properly verified through provision and management	Secure attribute repository	Attribute refresh frequency meets the system performance requirement; log for attribute changes and access	Log for attribute changes and access
Level 2	Includes Level 1 preparation; attributes' standard procedures and creation, update, and revoking policies are defined and documented	Includes Level 1 veracity; documented rule or standards for attribute value assignment and definition (syntax and semantic rule)	Includes Level 1 security; dedicated attribute repositories	Includes Level 1 readiness; attribute caching during run time meets the system performance requirement	Includes Level 1 management; attributes integrate with authentication
Level 3	N/A	N/A	Includes Level 2 security; transmission of attributes between access control functions should be protected from changing by any functions	Includes Level 2 readiness; fail-over or back-up attributes support; formal rules, policies, or standards for logging the creation, updates, modification, and deletion of attributes	N/A

NISTIR 8112, *Attribute Metadata: A Proposed Schema for Evaluating Federated Attributes* [3], explores veracity in terms of metadata and provides a guide for establishing a scoring framework and its associated components to enable standardized attribute confidence evaluations.

5.2 Attribute Practice Statement

Confidence in remote access control functions or attribute providers is gained by evaluating how secure the remote access control function or attribute provider's internal processes and procedures are with respect to both intentional attacks and unintentional errors or failures. It is often established on unverified assertions of validity that are not based on commonly agreed-upon standards. An example document that governs the effect of operations on attribute evaluation schemes is the Attribute Practice Statement (APS), which provides a listing of the attributes that will be used throughout the enterprise and may identify authoritative attribute sources for the enterprise. Still further network infrastructure capabilities (including the ability to maintain attribute veracity, security, and readiness) are required to share and replicate authoritative subject attribute data within and across organizations. For example, an Attribute Practice Statement can be based on a trust framework, such as NISTIR 8149, *Developing Trust Frameworks to Support Identity Federations* [18], for establishing the attribute evaluation scheme of veracity. The act of developing an auditable statement will provide an impartial assessment of the remote access control function or attribute provider's standards of operation as well as the confidence of the provided attribute. Thus, a higher attribute evaluation scheme level could be an APS that is audited for compliance with policy. Lower levels of an attribute evaluation scheme could apply to remote access control functions or attribute providers who self-report adherence to policy or do not publish their operation's practices.

6   Conclusions

An attribute-based access control system limits access to objects by evaluating rules against the attributes of entities (i.e., subject and object), operations, and the environment relevant to an access request and relies upon a formal relationship or access control rule that defines the allowable operations for subject/object attribute combinations. This document discusses considerations for attributes from the perspectives of fundamental assurance requirements: preparation, veracity, security, readiness, and management.

In addition to these considerations, a General Attribute Framework with accompanying examples is demonstrated to show the importance and efficiency of the semantic and syntactic accuracies of attributes in federated access control environments, especially when natural language policies are the initial policies. Finally, the discussed considerations are summarized to illustrate attribute evaluation scheme examples which are applied to different security requirements. Clearly, attribute evaluation scheme framework development requires additional research and stakeholder outreach to the organizations that are using an attribute-based access control system.

Appendix A—XACML Implementation of Table 10 and 11

The Appendix lists the XACML translation of the OMB M-07-16 privacy rule [17].

```xml
<?xml version="1.0" encoding="UTF-8" ?>
- <Policy xmlns="urn:oasis:names:tc:xacml:2.0:policy:schema:os" PolicyId="GAF-
    sample1" RuleCombiningAlgId="urn:oasis:names:tc:xacml:1.0:rule-combining-
    algorithm:deny-overrides">
  <Description>XACML sample for generic attributes of an OMB M-06-16 privacy
    rule</Description>
  <Target />
- <Rule Effect="Permit" RuleId="OMB M-06-16 Privacy rule">
  <Description>Grant Read access for the user who has the attributes: Remote User,
    Federal Agencies, and 2- factor (Level 3) to the resource data with the PII
    attributes.</Description>
- <Target>
- <Subjects>
- <Subject>
- <SubjectMatch MatchId="urn:oasis:names:tc:xacml:1.0:function:boolean-equal">
  <AttributeValue
      DataType="http://www.w3.org/2001/XMLSchema#boolean">True</AttributeValue
      >
  <SubjectAttributeDesignator AttributeId=""Remote Login ID""
      DataType="http://www.w3.org/2001/XMLSchema#boolean" MustBePresent="true"
      />
      </SubjectMatch>
- <SubjectMatch MatchId="urn:oasis:names:tc:xacml:1.0:function:boolean-equal">
  <AttributeValue
      DataType="http://www.w3.org/2001/XMLSchema#boolean">True</AttributeValue
      >
  <SubjectAttributeDesignator AttributeId=""Federal Agency""
      DataType="http://www.w3.org/2001/XMLSchema#boolean" MustBePresent="true"
      />
      </SubjectMatch>
- <SubjectMatch MatchId="urn:oasis:names:tc:xacml:1.0:function:boolean-equal">
  <AttributeValue
      DataType="http://www.w3.org/2001/XMLSchema#boolean">True</AttributeValue
      >
  <SubjectAttributeDesignator AttributeId=""2- factor (Level 3)""
      DataType="http://www.w3.org/2001/XMLSchema#boolean" MustBePresent="true"
      />
      </SubjectMatch>
      </Subject>
      </Subjects>
- <Resources>
- <Resource>
- <ResourceMatch MatchId="urn:oasis:names:tc:xacml:1.0:function:boolean-equal">
  <AttributeValue
      DataType="http://www.w3.org/2001/XMLSchema#boolean">True</AttributeValue
      >
```

```xml
  <ResourceAttributeDesignator AttributeId=""PII""
      DataType="http://www.w3.org/2001/XMLSchema#boolean" MustBePresent="true"
      />
      </ResourceMatch>
      </Resource>
      </Resources>
- <Actions>
- <Action>
- <ActionMatch MatchId="urn:oasis:names:tc:xacml:1.0:function:string-equal">
  <AttributeValue
      DataType="http://www.w3.org/2001/XMLSchema#string">Read</AttributeValue>
  <ActionAttributeDesignator AttributeId="urn:oasis:names:tc:xacml:1.0:action:action-id"
      DataType="http://www.w3.org/2001/XMLSchema#string" MustBePresent="true" />
      </ActionMatch>
      </Action>
      </Actions>
      </Target>
      </Rule>
      </Policy>
```

Appendix B—References

[1]   Hu VC, Ferraiolo DF, Kuhn R, Schnitzer A, Sandlin K, Miller R, Scarfone KA (2014)
Guide to Attribute Based Access Control (ABAC) Definition and Considerations.
(National Institute of Standards and Technology, Gaithersburg, MD), NIST Special
Publication (SP) 800-162, Includes updates as of February 25, 2019.
https://doi.org/10.6028/NIST.SP.800-162

[2]   InterNational Committee for Information Technology Standards (INCITS) (2018)
Information technology – Next Generation Access Control – Functional Architecture
(NGAC-FA).   (INCITS,   Washington,   DC),   INCITS   499-2018.
https://webstore.ansi.org/Standards/INCITS/INCITS4992018

[3]   Grassi PA, Lefkovitz NB, Nadeau EM, Galluzzo RJ, Dinh AT (2018) Attribute Metadata:
A Proposed Schema for Evaluating Federated Attributes. (National Institute of Standards
and Technology, Gaithersburg, MD), NIST Interagency or Internal Report (NISTIR) 8112.
https://doi.org/10.6028/NIST.IR.8112

[4]   Hu VC, Ferraiolo, DF, Kuhn DR (2006) Assessment of Access Control Systems. (National
Institute of Standards and Technology, Gaithersburg, MD), NIST Interagency or Internal
Report (NISTIR) 7316. https://doi.org/10.6028/NIST.IR.7316

[5]   Hu VC, Scarfone K (2012) Guidelines for Access Control System Evaluation Metrics.
(National Institute of Standards and Technology, Gaithersburg, MD), NIST Interagency or
Internal Report (NISTIR) 7874. https://doi.org/10.6028/NIST.IR.7874

[6]   Ferraiolo DF, Hu VC, Kuhn R, Chandramouli R (2016) A Comparison of Attribute Based
Access Control (ABAC) Standards for Data Service Applications: Extensible Access
Control Markup Language (XACML) and Next Generation Access Control (NGAC).
(National Institute of Standards and Technology, Gaithersburg, MD), NIST Special
Publication (SP) 800-178. https://doi.org/10.6028/NIST.SP.800-178

[7]   Office of Management and Budget (2003) E-Authentication Guidance for Federal
Agencies. (The White House, Washington, DC), OMB Memorandum M-04-04, December
16, 2003. Available at
https://www.whitehouse.gov/sites/whitehouse.gov/files/omb/memoranda/2004/m04-
04.pdf

[8]   Global Justice Information Sharing Initiative (Global) Security Working Group (2008)
Global Federated Identity and Privilege Management (GFIPM) Metadata Overview
Version 1.0. (U.S. Department of Justice, Washington, DC). Available at
https://it.ojp.gov/document-library

[9]   National Identity Exchange Federation (NIEF) (2019) *NIEF Attribute Repository*.
Available at https://nief.org/attribute-registry/index.html

[10]   OASIS (2019) *OASIS Security Services (SAML) TC*. Available at https://www.oasis-
open.org/committees/tc_home.php?wg_abbrev=security

[11]   Dierks T, Rescorla E (2018) The Transport Layer Security (TLS) Protocol Version 1.3. (Internet Engineering Task Force), IETF Request for Comments (RFC) 8446. https://doi.org/10.17487/RFC8446

[12]   Organization for the Advancement of Structured Information Standards (OASIS) (2019) *OASIS eXtensible Access Control Markup Language (XACML) TC.* Available at https://www.oasis-open.org/committees/xacml/

[13]   Bhatt S, Patwa F, Sandhu R (2017) ABAC with Group Attributes and Attribute Hierarchies Utilizing the Policy Machine. *Proceedings of the 2nd ACM Workshop on Attribute Based Access Control (ABAC 2017)*, (ACM, Scottsdale, AZ), pp 17-28. https://doi.org/10.1145/3041048.3041053

[14]   Biswas P, Sandhu R, Krishnan R (2017) Attribute Transformation for Attribute-Based Access Control. *Proceedings of the 2nd ACM Workshop on Attribute-Based Access Control (ABAC 2017)*, (ACM, Scottsdale, AZ), pp 1-8. https://doi.org/10.1145/3041048.3041052

[15]   Hindle A (2014) *Authentication vs. Authorization – Part 1: Federated Authentication.* (Axiomatics). Available at https://www.axiomatics.com/blog/authentication-vs-authorization-part-1-federated-authentication-2/

[16]   Office of Management and Budget (2006) Protection of Sensitive Agency Information. (The White House, Washington, DC), OMB Memorandum M-06-16, June 23, 2006. Available at https://www.whitehouse.gov/sites/whitehouse.gov/files/omb/memoranda/2006/m06-16.pdf

[17]   Office of Management and Budget (2007) Safeguarding Against and Responding to the Breach of Personally Identifiable Information. (The White House, Washington, DC), OMB Memorandum M-07-16, May 22, 2007. Available at https://www.whitehouse.gov/sites/whitehouse.gov/files/omb/memoranda/2007/m07-16.pdf

[18]   Temoshok D, Abruzzi C (2018) Developing Trust Frameworks to Support Identity Federations. (National Institute of Standards and Technology, Gaithersburg, MD), NIST Interagency or Internal Report (NISTIR) 8149. https://doi.org/10.6028/NIST.IR.8149

www.ingramcontent.com/pod-product-compliance
Lightning Source LLC
Chambersburg PA
CBHW060509060326
40689CB00020B/4689